Urban Fledgling

by

Annie Cowell

First published 2026 by The Hedgehog Poetry Press

Published in the UK by
The Hedgehog Poetry Press
5, Coppack House
Churchill Avenue
Clevedon
BS21 6QW

www.hedgehogpress.co.uk

ISBN: 978-1-916830-59-2

Copyright © Annie Cowell 2026

The right of Annie Cowell to be identified as the author of this work has been asserted in accordance with the Copyright, Designs and Patents Act 1988.

All rights reserved. No part of this publication may be reproduced, stored in or introduced into a retrieval system, or transmitted in any form, or by any means (electronic, mechanical, photocopying, recording or otherwise) without prior written permissions of the publisher. Any person who does any unauthorised act in relation to this publication may be liable for criminal prosecution and civil claims for damages.

9 8 7 6 5 4 3 2 1

A CIP Catalogue record for this book is available from the British Library.

For Stuart

'I know from experience that the poets are right: love is eternal.'*

*E. M Forster

Contents

I label the swallows' nest fragile 7

Morning commute 8

Church Grim 9

Rookie 10

Summer Leaves, falling 11

Street Art 12

Slugged 13

The pub cat is dead 14

Ode to mallards and a baccy tin 15

Moon over PAU• 16

Balm 17

The Fox at open mic 18

The man in the cafe is crying 19

I'm rereading Wilfred Owen	20
Story time is cancelled	21
Let the spiders in.	22
Cold moon murmur	24
Family kitchen signs	25
Spud.	26
February Fairmaids	27
The march of the *martoui*.	28
The truth about cows	30
Swing Song	31
Timekeeper	32
Puttering	33
A Thin Place	34

I LABEL THE SWALLOWS' NEST FRAGILE

pack it with bougainvillea petals
lemons, olives, pomegranates,
tuck it away in my heart.
Beneath my skin, infused with lavender,
molecules of sand and dust are stored.
The space behind my eyes is full
of blue firmament, speckled with flights
of swallows. I have memorised
their giddy shrieking
the evening chorus of cicadas,
the scuttling of the lizards;
I will replay their melodies
to mute the din of cars and wailing sirens
as I unpack my life under a pigeon sky.
The moon I have tethered
to a thread of light;
we will wax and wane together,
unravelled in the darkness of city nights.

MORNING COMMUTE

It is so early
that there are only the wild things.
Predawn a fox crosses my path,
bloodied back leg held close. His white tail
waves surrender as he disappears. Overnight,
a tent has sprouted beneath the trees
where a man's shadow billows cold smoke
How long before his tent is uprooted
and replanted elsewhere
I wonder as I scurry past growling squirrels
who have taken over the playground?
grey clings over everything- the light, the fluster
of pigeons fussing over dead bread
left by rats who lurk in the damp undergrowth
waiting, like me, for a chink of sunlight.

CHURCH GRIM

By day he is a smudge on the pavement
outside M and S. This black, three legged dog shares
a space with the homeless man who leans against
the wall.   always a gap   between them, the dog,
with gnarled joints and filthy fur
refuses the blanket the man lays out for him -
prefers, it seems, to own the slab.
At dusk the man packs his bags and moves
to the graveyard behind the tower. His grey head
bobs like the moon and the dog hops behind him,
 a dark cloud, untethered
yet held by a thread of light. Strangers will whisper
of a hound glimpsed in the churchyard's dark crevices,
imagining Black Shuck, or some such demon cur.
But the dog and his man sleep in soft green
between the graves, eased perhaps by grassy arias,
spectral fingers of ground elder and scents of wild garlic
whilst locals turn a blind eye on their church grim
and the man who lives beside him.

ROOKIE

There's an intruder in my kitchen.
Duped by a twinkle a bird has fluttered
through my open door
towards a mirage.
A rookie error to be fooled by a mirror.
Now it is trapped; the door elusive,
the windows closed.
It bashes against glass, leaves a bloody smudge,
becomes a squawking mess of shit and feathers.
My dogs wake, hackles rising.
They fire barks, round after round, pause, reload.
The fledgling pants, spent on my draining board.
Its terrified heart beats in my throat
but I swallow our fear
unlatch the window,
send it flapping to the faultless sky.

SUMMER LEAVES, FALLING

On the hottest day of the year,
London aches like an inflamed
boil itching to be lanced.
We join the masses oozing onto its streets,
pass sleeping rats stilled between blades
of brittle sage and leak
towards a park in search of trees.
Summer's zenith, but the trees bleed
parched foliage;
summer leaves, falling.
The city feels ablaze; fuelled by
the steady drip, drip, drip
of dry leaves falling

The park, balding, is drenched in sodden
bodies; high on heat
they huddle in sweaty clusters, cavorting
on blankets, dogs panting, bodies
red, smoking...
spilling dregs of beer, Prosecco bottles
tipped onto chapped soil.
Thirsty. We wedge on the edge of shadow
neath a plane tree where the hard ground
pokes our creaking bones.
(*What did you expect?*) The tree's roots
buried so deep in our past
are exposed, naked as the crimson bodies,
except where its dry leaves gather.
Summer leaves,
falling.

STREET ART

Tree and sunlight have conspired
to paint a window on the pavement.
It glows, this buttercup portal
like a stain glass opening
to another world.
the street becomes a pop up
gallery - people pause   mid   step

phones
poised, clicking

Later, they will browse
a host of yellow,
wonder at green tendrils
like tiny veins, graze fingertips
over paving stone
cracks like calmes
bruised by footfall

SLUGGED

Found, flaccid,
amongst my greens,
I scooped you on the shovel's tip
and lobbed you over the wall.
Repulsive as a toddler with a snotty nose
I was relieved to be rid.
Next day, tiny teeth had left their
mark on every shoot. Declaring war
I crushed egg shells and scattered them like a fortress -
imagined moist flesh tearing.
Yet still you came, and now at dusk
I bury a crock in the soil and fill it with beer.
'Fool proof' my neighbour said,
promising death in its sweetness.
Later, cocooned in sleep
a baby's foot withers
and I awake, gulping.
Your crystal trail glistens
with a duper's delight -
mocking my attempts at victory.
A single cabbage survives the skirmishes.
Nurtured to maturity;
picked with pride.
And when at last
I slice my prize
you are there
nestled
deep
inside.

THE PUB CAT IS DEAD

She, a black thread, wove
from table to table -
tapestry maker
patching people together.
young, all fur and purr,
rubbed legs, a head to scratch
she danced onto laps
kneading, kneading.
Old, all hiss and claws, reclusive,
shadow dweller
street cat,
fighter,
survivor
long after others came and went.
for a score of years
a regular, a celebrity, the glue.

ODE TO MALLARDS AND A BACCY TIN

the lid, sleek as a mallard's head
golden and green
loosened
the loamy mulch scent
of Sunday mornings
in the park.
Dad held the bag of bread,
whilst I tossed chunks to clacking beaks,
ignoring the first greedy marauders,
aiming for the smallest -
the one at the edge, nervous,
beaten to every crumb by bigger birds.

Later, when dad opened his baccy tin
and teased saffron threads
from the woody nest inside,
I would watch, bewitched, as he
rolled and coaxed the baccy
into shape, marvelling at his fingers'
dexterity. The quick lick of the Rizla,
first inhalation and breathless wait
for him to mouth smoky bagels
towards me.
They would float uncatchable,
fade
disappear,
while I pecked,
like a hungry mallard,
feeding on crumbs.

MOON OVER PAU •

Blinded by fluorescence
we float, as if cast adrift.
Time here ticks by in the ebb
and flow of footsteps, beeping monitors
untouched coffees...
We hold our breath, pulled under
as we count your rough inhalations
and I repeat -
When you are better, I will be better..
A mantra. A bargain.
Almost a prayer.
The window yawns, a black hole
in which the moon's full face
stares like an angel whose lips
blow a kiss, recite a psalm.
She knows we all came from the stars,
knows we will return to the stars.
But for now, we are pinpricks of light
holding on by our fingertips -
two souls
anchored to the world.

• paediatric assessment unit

BALM

There is balm in the park.
I lap it like a fox
from green puddles of sun and shade
under the trees in the walled garden.
The blackbird, now familiar, lingers
with me, shares the tree's exhalations.
Today, as I pause on the bench
wood warm from sun, a rustle of red
reveals a robin. It darts from grassy
shadow to where I sit, stays a second
to hold me in its glassy stare.
It is a messenger from generations past

A sign that all will be well.

THE FOX AT OPEN MIC

On this last night of summer
the air buzzes in a walled city garden
as poets' voices fizz and crackle,
like a broken radio
searching for the right frequency.
As we listen, each trying to find the music
in another's cadence
he hovers like the first autumn leaf,
a russet glisk in the shadows.
He circles our edges with his red brush
before taking centre stage.

We pause
dazzled by the feral rizz
of his essence.

The words we sacrificed are lost.
the meanings
we sought are here
caught
in his heroic silence.

THE MAN IN THE CAFE IS CRYING

I am in the queue
choosing between pink pancakes
and bibimbap when he begins.
Half eaten hiccups become
loud guttural sobs.
The sound pulls the queue taut.
It is Sunday morning and his cries
hit hard like the first slug of coffee.
He leans against the cake cabinet
face red, tears streaming.

What's wrong, what's wrong?

His answer incomprehensible
choking.
Gentle hands guide him to a seat,
administer coffee. Between sips the crying subsides.

In his silence, Sunday morning returns
and we all go about our business.

I'M REREADING WILFRED OWEN

News of war snipes at us
from tv, radio, social media
images whistling past like bullets
as we tune in and scroll down
so much *exposure* -
we donate, collect, protest, pray
knowing that it's not enough.
I re read Wilfred Owen
read the spaces between his words
knowing that if words cannot win wars
what is the point
imagine there are poets warring now
battling to decide which truths they should reveal
a new 'Anthem for the Doomed Youth', perhaps?
Will they speak of one small man
his finger poised in threat
or will they write of young men returning,
discarding ballet shoes and tennis rackets,
following their leading actor, unrehearsed, onto the stage.
Or of mothers making molotov cocktails,
women offering handfuls of sunflower seeds
whilst their children grow in darkness underground -
A nation forced once more into believing
Dulce et decorum est
Pro patria mori

STORY TIME IS CANCELLED

the librarian tells us.
Short staffed, she explains
retreating.
No one moves. We wait.
toddlers hurl books from shelves
unknowing, we become a protest
No one will move without story time.
We have come to hear about sharks
in parks and ketchup on tomatoes and to sing
How can we move unless we sing?
We need the bus wheels to go
round and round, the little star
to twinkle, the sleeping bunnies
to wake.
The librarian returns
Here, she says, *I will release the animals*
and places the bag on the mat
like a sacrifice. small hands free
cows and cats and ducks and
lions and giraffes from their darkness
whilst adults hum tunes
in their heads.

LET THE SPIDERS IN

In this coldest winter
I will turn the heating down,
share blankets with the moths.
When the first fingers of ice tap
at my window I will loose the latch
and let the spiders in.
Together, we will mimic the bees,
bed down for a brumal slumber party.
As the leaves tumble, let them gather
in a blazing eiderdown for the cold soil;
let the beetles, mice and hogs clamber under.

In this leanest winter
I will disconnect the cooker,
let the fridge become a void,
consumed with emptiness.
I will keep my milk outside
where sparrows can peck holes
for pink tongues to dip inside.
I shall exhume potatoes, desperate arms
sprouting from the coffin of my cupboard,
bury them in the garden to rest
until the spring will give them life again.

In this darkest winter,
I will keep the lights turned off,
draw back the curtains
so that my insect guests and I
can binge on nightly episodes of the moon.
As she dons the robes of Hunter, Beaver, Wolf,
supported by her cast of lesser stars;
Orion, Gemini, The Bear and Dragon
we will shiver at their stellar performances
illuminating long hours of blackness
with their lunar brilliance.

In this cruellest winter
we can be kind. We can open our doors
and let the spiders in.

COLD MOON MURMUR

As the moon lifts her swollen self
into the dulling sky,
some ancient stirring pulls me
to the wilderness, where, like an augur,
I root myself beside the reeds
and watch for auspices.

The air buzzes, crackles with interference
then breaks like waves on a pebble beach.
A squalling mass of starlings flood the sky,
each an equal note in the movement. They bend
and twist; first a dark sun eclipsing the moon,
now a swan, a funnel, a fish -
pixelating the dusk with calligraphic messages.

We are connected;
the beating of their wings, the dance, the song
the beating of my heart,
a fluttering signal.

A murmur.

FAMILY KITCHEN SIGNS

*Please help us keep this room tidy
by cleaning up after yourselves*

*Please do not leave your food
in the microwave unattended*

*Please do not walk on the ward
with hot drinks unless covered*

*Due to infection control policies
food stored in this fridge must
be labelled with date and name
and must not be in plastic bags*

*Makaton signs of the month
are for toilet and thank you.*

Thank you for your co operation

On the ward,
my son and grandson are folded together
in a cot, an odd origami bird
sleeping

SPUD

There is a smell of death.
Black eyes stare from the cupboard
where a bruised body lurks.
A solitary spud.
It can't be eaten now-
green, fetid, reeking of damp moss
and anyway
the cooker is disconnected and
so is the fridge.
Its door is ajar, like a mouth
asking why?
It's dark inside.
Empty.
The house is cold enough
to keep milk chilled-
if there was milk
Boxes of cereal in the pantry,
tins of soup and beans are
cold comfort.
The dead potato reaches out
to me, arms sprouting
from its decomposing corpse.
I will bury it in the garden.
Maybe the sun will pull
those arms through to the light
and it will live again.

FEBRUARY FAIRMAIDS

In the grey mizzle of dusk
some green girls have gathered
under a tree in the park.
Bowed heads under white bonnets,
faces hidden, small groups
of ghostly figures, nodding.
Too fragile to stand
barefoot in the wet grass
I fear they won't survive the night,
that tomorrow their withered carcasses
will lie crumpled amongst dripping blades.
Yet come the morn my pensive steps
find that they have multiplied.
Tiny candles piercing the hard earth
lighting the gloom of
another day

THE MARCH OF THE *MARTOUI*

Each spring
you tear
your candy
floss nest
and pour
like burnt
sugar strands
from a
boiling pan
drip
drip
a brown trail
armed with
orange hairs
poisoned harpoons
you hurl
on the breeze
deadly to
curious dogs
you are
- it's said -
an ill omen
marching
nosetotail
no carnival
more soldiers
invading or
funeral cortege
and while
green sprouts
to sunlight

you tunnel
underground
to darkness
burrow deep
until the day
when you
emerge
spectral.

THE TRUTH ABOUT COWS

I've heard a lot of bad stuff about cows;
about how these murderous brutes
are hell bent on killing people, one way or another.
I've read about the dog walkers
gangs of cows have trampled to death;
of how those burgers we gobble
will fester in our bowels,
the milk we guzzle make us sick.
I've heard about how cows are burping
and farting methane willy nilly
into our air, turning up the temperature,
killing our planet.

So, when a bunch of the beasts move
into a field near my house, I watch
for signs of bother.
I notice how they chew and chew and chew,
gooey threads hanging from mouths
dotted with flies like currant buns.
I notice their soft brown eyes; curious
how they stand with faces gentled by the sun,
sisters, leaning into each other.
I watch them canter on dew-soaked mornings,
kicking up hooves in moist grass,
lying down later, as they smell the rain.
Their lowing lulls like a Greek chorus;
though they are the protagonists.
It is our hubris which prevents us
from seeing the truth about cows;
from seeing we are the villains
in this tragedy.

What is the truth about cows?

They are a poem in compassion. *

* Mahatma Gandhi

SWING SONG

On the swing, you are just a boy.
                        Legs out, head flung back
w*hoosh* and up
                        whoop and down
free from falling
                        too soon from the nest
you are just a boy on a swing.
                        Legs out, head flung back
the sky is a smile
                        that matches your own.
You're a bee, a bird, a butterfly
                        rocket, plane, shooting
   star.
                        w*hoosh* and up
w*hoop* and down
                        Just a boy on a swing who is
   you.

TIMEKEEPER

Born on a breath; a feathery
will o' the wisp
you flutter on breezes.
Collector of broken - winged ladybirds,
lost dogs, lost souls
fragile as spring's first snowdrop;
fearless as the sun.
A shadow slayer.
Your heart beats, daughter,
keep time with my own.

PUTTERING

I have a head crammed
with the clutter of
climate and conflict.
A flotsam of daily detritus
where my mind flounders.
I need a life - belt
so I'm learning how to putter.
Breakfast is a ritual of kettle, cup, tea;
the first bitter -sweet sip of the day,
tannin on tongue.
I hang the laundry with precision,
noting the skuttering of a robin
as it darts from sun to shadow,
I savour the bend and stretch,
the warm dampness
of clean clothes, the wooden peg pinched between
thumb and fingers.
I wallow in the hedonism
of washing dishes, warm soapy water
temperature tested as if for a newborn,
each dish a gift of mindless concentration.
no room to think - just putter, putter
Today, as the latest news
of floods, fires, bombs, deaths explodes
I will pursue the perfect pleasure
of polishing my dirty panes.
With spray and cloth I'll clean
the broken pieces of myself together.

A THIN PLACE

If you walk in a straight line across the beach
from the footpath which runs between
blue mountain and the graveyard,
past the marram mounds, dunes crawling with devils' toenails,
you will come to the spot where the seagulls settle
just before the water's edge.

If you stand in that spot,
feet in foam, toes tunnelling crustaceans,
put the steelwork's skeleton behind you
and let your gaze wander to Huntcliffe;
even in greyest fret a pink gossamer glimmers
shrouding land sea and sky.

If you linger, time will rest with you.
The glow mutes the din of ebb and flow -
silence gifts serendipity -pin pricks of sound -
a dog barking, children laughing.
The veil hides nothing here;
worlds are visible in breaths and heart beats.

If you turn, like the gulls, to the sunshine-
shadows lengthen in your wake.
A cold bluster will blast the morass
as you empty the dust from your pockets -

Hope can happen in a moment
here.

In this thin place.

www.ingramcontent.com/pod-product-compliance
Lightning Source LLC
Chambersburg PA
CBHW021640080526
44584CB00015BA/1617